AI Tomorrow
Navigating the Future

Understanding AI's Impact on Jobs, Society, and Ethics

Introduction

Welcome to "The Future with Artificial Intelligence"! In this book, we will delve into how artificial intelligence (AI) is transforming our world, replacing traditional professions, reshaping the job market, and creating new opportunities for humanity. We will explore which professions are at risk, which new skills will become essential, and how we can harness the power of AI to enhance our lives and careers.

What is Artificial Intelligence?

Artificial intelligence refers to the field of computer science aimed at creating machines capable of performing tasks that typically require human intelligence. This includes abilities such as learning, speech recognition, problem-solving, data analysis, and even creative tasks like generating music or art.

AI can be categorized into several levels:

- **Narrow AI (ANI):** Specialized in performing one task or a set of tasks. Examples include voice assistants like Siri and Alexa, which can follow commands but do not possess general knowledge.
- **General AI (AGI):** Capable of performing any intellectual task that a human can. Currently, AGI remains a hypothetical concept, with many researchers working towards it.

- **Superintelligence (ASI):** Surpasses human intelligence in all areas. ASI is the subject of many scientific and philosophical discussions about the future of humanity.

History and Development of AI

The history of AI begins with philosophical considerations of what intelligence is and whether it can be replicated. Practical steps were taken in the mid-20th century.

- **1950s:** Alan Turing proposed the Turing Test to evaluate a machine's ability to exhibit human-like intelligence. In 1956, the term "artificial intelligence" was officially introduced at the Dartmouth Conference.
- **1960s-70s:** Early AI programs like ELIZA modeled simple conversations. Expert systems were developed to perform specialized tasks.
- **1980s:** Advances in machine learning and the development of algorithms capable of learning from data.
- **1990s:** The development of neural networks and deep learning algorithms led to significant breakthroughs in pattern recognition and natural language processing.
- **2000s and beyond:** The explosive growth of AI due to increased computational power and data availability. Modern achievements include autonomous vehicles, intelligent voice assistants, and recommendation systems.

Modern Achievements of AI

AI has already transformed many aspects of our lives and continues to advance rapidly. Let's consider some key areas where AI has shown significant success:

1. Medicine AI is used for diagnosing diseases, predicting epidemics, and developing personalized treatment plans. For example, AI systems can analyze medical images to detect cancer at early stages with accuracy surpassing that of humans.

2. Finance AI helps manage investments, assess risks, and detect fraud. Trading algorithms can analyze vast amounts of data and make decisions in fractions of a second, which is beyond human capability.

3. Education Personalized learning programs based on AI can adapt to each student's needs, improving learning outcomes. Online platforms like Coursera and Khan Academy use AI to analyze student progress and recommend educational materials.

4. Transportation Autonomous vehicles, such as cars and drones, are becoming a reality thanks to AI. They can analyze the environment and make real-time decisions, improving safety and efficiency.

5. Entertainment AI is used in the creation of films, music, and video games. For instance, AI can generate scripts, compose music, and create realistic characters for video games.

The Impact of AI on Society

AI has a significant impact on society, both positive and negative. Positive aspects include increased efficiency, improved quality of life, and new business opportunities.

However, there are challenges such as job displacement, data privacy issues, and ethical dilemmas.

1. Job Displacement Many professions may be automated, leading to job loss. However, AI also creates new professions that require new skills.

2. Data Privacy The collection and analysis of big data raise privacy and security concerns. Laws and norms need to be developed to protect personal data.

3. Ethical Dilemmas AI can make decisions with significant ethical implications. It is crucial to develop ethical principles and guidelines for using AI.

The Future of AI

The future of AI promises to be exciting and full of opportunities. Technology will continue to develop, and AI will be integrated into all aspects of our lives. We can expect smarter systems that help us solve complex problems, improve our quality of life, and open new horizons.

However, it is necessary to prepare for future changes. Learning new skills, adapting to new conditions, and understanding the ethical aspects of using AI will become key elements of successful coexistence with AI.

In the following chapters, we will explore how AI is replacing traditional professions, what new opportunities it creates, how to learn and work together with AI, and what ethical questions need to be considered.

Chapter 1: The Replacement of Jobs by AI

Artificial intelligence (AI) is revolutionizing many aspects of our lives and continues to develop at a rapid pace. One of the most significant transformations brought about by AI is the replacement of traditional jobs. In this chapter, we will explore which professions are most at risk, examine examples of how machines are already replacing humans in various industries, and discuss the broader implications for the labor market and society.

Professions at Risk

As AI and automation technologies advance, many jobs, especially those involving routine tasks, are at risk of being replaced. Let's delve into some examples of professions that are most vulnerable to AI and automation:

1. Manufacturing Workers Manufacturing jobs, particularly those involving repetitive tasks, are among the first to be automated. Modern factories increasingly employ robotic systems to perform tasks such as welding, assembly, and packaging. Companies like Tesla use robots extensively in their production lines, reducing the need for human workers.

2. Cashiers and Retail Workers Automated checkout systems and self-service kiosks are becoming more common in retail stores. Shops like Amazon Go have implemented technology that allows customers to pick up items and leave the store without going through a traditional checkout, thus reducing the need for cashiers.

3. Logistics and Transportation Autonomous vehicles and drones are poised to replace drivers and delivery personnel. Companies like Waymo and Amazon are developing and testing self-driving trucks and delivery drones, which can transport goods more efficiently and at a lower cost.

4. Accountants and Auditors AI-powered software can handle many accounting tasks, such as transaction processing, report generation, and auditing. Tools like QuickBooks and Xero are already automating much of the accounting work for small businesses, reducing the demand for human accountants.

5. Legal Assistants AI can analyze large volumes of legal documents and find relevant information much faster than a human can. Programs like ROSS Intelligence use natural language processing to search through legal precedents and case law, which can significantly reduce the need for paralegals.

6. Journalists and Copywriters Automated content generation tools are capable of writing news articles and reports based on data inputs. The Washington Post uses an AI system called Heliograf to produce short news articles and updates, allowing human journalists to focus on more complex stories.

7. Medical Professionals While AI cannot fully replace doctors, it is being used for many diagnostic tasks.

Systems like IBM Watson can analyze medical data, diagnose diseases, and suggest treatment options, allowing doctors to concentrate on more complicated cases. AI tools are also being used to assist in radiology and pathology by analyzing medical images for signs of disease.

Examples of Human Replacement by Machines

The automotive industry provides a clear example of human replacement by machines. For instance, at Tesla's factories, robots perform most of the work in assembling cars, including welding, painting, and installing components. This extensive use of robotics has significantly reduced the number of workers needed on the production line while increasing productivity and efficiency.

In the retail sector, companies like Walmart and Amazon are heavily investing in automated systems. Amazon Go stores use advanced sensors and cameras to track what customers pick up, automatically charging their accounts as they leave the store. This eliminates the need for cashiers and speeds up the shopping experience.

In the logistics and transportation industry, Amazon and UPS are actively testing drones for package delivery. These drones can deliver goods faster and more cost-effectively than traditional delivery methods, reducing the need for human couriers and drivers.

The Impact of AI on the Labor Market

The implementation of AI in the labor market has both positive and negative consequences. On the positive side, automation can increase efficiency and productivity, reduce costs, and improve service quality. On the negative side, the replacement of human labor with machines can lead to mass unemployment and social issues.

1. Increased Productivity Automating routine tasks allows companies to increase productivity and reduce costs. This is particularly relevant in manufacturing and logistics, where robots can work faster and more accurately than humans.

2. Improved Service Quality AI can enhance the quality of services provided by companies. For example, AI systems can analyze customer data and offer personalized recommendations, leading to higher customer satisfaction.

3. Social and Economic Issues The replacement of human labor with machines can lead to mass unemployment, especially among workers performing routine tasks. This can cause social and economic problems, such as increased inequality and a decline in living standards.

Adapting to Changes

To successfully adapt to the changes brought about by AI, it is essential to develop new skills and be prepared for shifts in the labor market. Here are some steps that can help with adaptation:

1. Learning New Skills Continuous learning and development of new skills will be critical for a successful career in the future. Courses and programs in AI, machine learning, and data analytics can help individuals remain competitive in the labor market.

2. Adapting to New Conditions Flexibility and readiness to adapt will help individuals successfully navigate new conditions. This includes being willing to retrain and acquire new professions.

3. Using AI to Improve Work Using AI and automation to enhance work and increase productivity will become an essential skill. This involves mastering tools and technologies that help automate routine tasks and focus on more complex and creative tasks.

Conclusion

AI has a profound impact on the labor market and society as a whole. While many traditional professions are at risk of being replaced, AI also opens up new opportunities and creates jobs for the future. Adapting to these changes requires learning new skills, understanding AI technologies, and being willing to collaborate with machines. In the following chapters, we will explore how to prepare for these changes, use AI to improve our lives and careers, and address the ethical issues that arise.

Chapter 2: Professions at Risk

Introduction

As artificial intelligence (AI) and automation technologies advance, many traditional professions are at risk of disappearing. Automating routine tasks allows companies to reduce costs and increase productivity, but it also leads to significant job losses. In this chapter, we will explore which professions are most at risk and discuss how these changes might impact the labor market and society as a whole.

Professions at Risk of Automation

1. Manufacturing Workers

Manufacturing workers performing routine and repetitive tasks are among the first to be replaced. Modern factories increasingly use robotic systems to perform tasks such as welding, assembly, and packaging.

Example: Companies like Tesla extensively use robots in their manufacturing processes, significantly reducing the need for workers on the production line while increasing productivity and efficiency.

2. Cashiers and Retail Workers

Automated checkout systems and self-service kiosks are becoming more common in retail stores. These systems allow customers to scan and pay for items themselves, reducing the need for cashiers.

Example: Amazon Go stores utilize advanced sensors and cameras that allow customers to pick up items and leave the store without going through a traditional checkout, eliminating the need for cashiers and speeding up the shopping experience.

3. Logistics and Transportation

Autonomous vehicles and drones are set to replace drivers and delivery personnel. Companies like Waymo and Amazon are developing and testing self-driving trucks and delivery drones, which can transport goods more efficiently and at a lower cost.

Example: Amazon and UPS are actively testing delivery drones, which can deliver packages faster and more cost-effectively than traditional delivery methods, reducing the need for human couriers and drivers.

4. Accountants and Auditors

AI-powered software can handle many accounting tasks, such as transaction processing, report generation, and auditing. Tools like QuickBooks and Xero are automating much of the accounting work for small businesses, reducing the demand for human accountants.

Example: AI systems can automatically classify expenses and revenues, identify errors, and alert auditors to potential risks, significantly reducing the need for manual accounting tasks.

5. Legal Assistants

AI can analyze large volumes of legal documents and find relevant information much faster than a human can. Programs like ROSS Intelligence use natural language processing to search through legal precedents and case law, which can significantly reduce the need for paralegals.

Example: AI systems can quickly sift through thousands of legal documents to find pertinent information, reducing the time and labor required by legal assistants and enabling lawyers to focus on higher-level tasks.

6. Journalists and Copywriters

Automated content generation tools are capable of writing news articles and reports based on data inputs. The Washington Post uses an AI system called Heliograf to produce short news articles and updates, allowing human journalists to focus on more complex stories.

Example: Automated systems can generate content such as sports summaries, financial reports, and even weather updates, reducing the need for human writers for routine reporting tasks.

7. Medical Professionals

While AI cannot fully replace doctors, it is being used for many diagnostic tasks. Systems like IBM Watson can analyze medical data, diagnose diseases, and suggest treatment options, allowing doctors to concentrate on more complicated cases. AI tools are also being used to assist in radiology and pathology by analyzing medical images for signs of disease.

Example: AI systems can analyze thousands of medical images in a fraction of the time it would take a human, identifying abnormalities with high accuracy and assisting doctors in making faster, more accurate diagnoses.

The Broader Impact on the Labor Market

The implementation of AI in the labor market has both positive and negative consequences. On the positive side, automation can increase efficiency and productivity, reduce costs, and improve service quality. On the negative side, the replacement of human labor with machines can lead to mass unemployment and social issues.

1. Increased Productivity

Automating routine tasks allows companies to increase productivity and reduce costs. This is particularly relevant in manufacturing and logistics, where robots can work faster and more accurately than humans.

2. Improved Service Quality

AI can enhance the quality of services provided by companies. For example, AI systems can analyze customer data and offer personalized recommendations, leading to higher customer satisfaction.

3. Social and Economic Issues

The replacement of human labor with machines can lead to mass unemployment, especially among workers performing routine tasks. This can cause social and economic problems, such as increased inequality and a decline in living standards.

Adapting to Changes

To successfully adapt to the changes brought about by AI, it is essential to develop new skills and be prepared for shifts in the labor market. Here are some steps that can help with adaptation:

1. Learning New Skills

Continuous learning and development of new skills will be critical for a successful career in the future. Courses and programs in AI, machine learning, and data analytics can help individuals remain competitive in the labor market.

2. Adapting to New Conditions

Flexibility and readiness to adapt will help individuals successfully navigate new conditions. This includes being willing to retrain and acquire new professions.

3. Using AI to Improve Work

Using AI and automation to enhance work and increase productivity will become an essential skill. This involves mastering tools and technologies that help automate routine tasks and focus on more complex and creative tasks.

Conclusion

AI has a profound impact on the labor market and society as a whole. While many traditional professions are at risk of being replaced, AI also opens up new opportunities and creates jobs for the future. Adapting to these changes requires learning new skills, understanding AI technologies, and being willing to collaborate with machines. In the following chapters, we will explore how to prepare for these changes, use AI to improve our lives and careers, and address the ethical issues that arise.

Chapter 3: Professions of the Future Created by AI

Introduction

While artificial intelligence (AI) threatens to replace many traditional jobs, it also opens the door to entirely new opportunities and professions. These new careers require unique skills and approaches that were not previously in demand. In this chapter, we will explore the new professions emerging due to AI and how they are reshaping our labor market and society.

Professions of the Future Created by AI

1. Machine Learning Specialists

With the increasing use of AI and machine learning (ML) in various industries, the demand for specialists in this field has grown significantly. Machine learning specialists develop algorithms and models that enable systems to learn and improve without explicit programming.

Key Skills:

- Linear algebra and statistics
- Learning algorithms (regression, classification, clustering)

- Data processing and analysis
- Programming languages such as Python and R
- Using libraries like TensorFlow and scikit-learn

Example: Machine learning specialists can work at companies like Google, developing algorithms to improve search query quality and recommendations. In healthcare, they can create models for diagnosing diseases based on medical images and patient data.

2. Robotics Engineers

Robotics is a rapidly growing field where engineers design, develop, and program robots to perform various tasks. Robotics engineers work on creating robots that can handle complex operations in manufacturing, healthcare, agriculture, and other industries.

Key Skills:

- Mechanics and electronics
- Robot control and navigation
- Signal processing and sensors
- Programming languages such as C++ and Python
- Using platforms like ROS (Robot Operating System)

Example: Robotics engineers can develop industrial robots for automotive factories like Tesla or medical robots that assist surgeons in performing minimally invasive operations.

3. Data Analysts

Data analysts play a crucial role in interpreting and analyzing large volumes of data generated by AI systems.

They help companies make informed decisions based on data insights, optimize business processes, and improve product and service quality.

Key Skills:

- Statistics and data visualization
- Programming for data analysis (Python, R)
- Data mining and cleaning
- Tools like SQL, Excel, Tableau

Example: Data analysts can work in marketing firms, analyzing consumer behavior to develop effective sales strategies. In finance, they can analyze market data to predict trends and manage risks.

4. Cybersecurity Specialists

With the growth of AI and the increase in data volumes, cybersecurity issues are becoming more relevant. Cybersecurity specialists develop and implement measures to prevent hacking, data theft, and other cyber threats. They also work on ensuring the security of AI systems and protecting sensitive information.

Key Skills:

- Cryptography and network security
- Methods for detecting and preventing attacks
- Ensuring data confidentiality
- Developing secure AI algorithms

Example: Cybersecurity specialists can work in large corporations like Microsoft, developing security measures for cloud services and preventing cyberattacks. In finance, they can protect banking systems and prevent fraud.

5. AI Developers

AI developers create algorithms and systems that use AI technologies to solve various tasks. They work on improving existing technologies and developing new solutions for different industries. AI developers need deep knowledge in computer science, programming, and mathematics.

Key Skills:

- AI algorithms and models
- Programming languages (Python, Java)
- Data structures and algorithms
- Using AI frameworks (TensorFlow, PyTorch)

Example: AI developers can work in companies developing autonomous vehicles like Waymo, creating systems that enable cars to navigate roads independently. In healthcare, they can develop algorithms for analyzing medical images and patient data.

6. AI Ethicists

As AI develops, many ethical issues arise regarding its use. AI ethicists develop principles and norms that help guide technology development in an ethical direction. They study AI's impact on society, privacy issues, discrimination, and other ethical aspects.

Key Skills:

- Ethics and philosophy
- Knowledge of AI technologies
- Critical thinking and analysis
- Communication and policy development

Example: AI ethicists can work in research centers and universities, developing ethical principles for AI use in various industries. They can also consult companies like Google and Facebook on ethical use of AI technologies.

The Impact of New Professions on the Labor Market

The creation of new AI-related professions has a significant impact on the labor market and society. These changes lead to new opportunities, higher skill requirements, and shifts in employment structure.

1. New Opportunities

New AI-related professions open up numerous opportunities for people with diverse skills and interests. This includes both technical and non-technical roles such as data analysts, cybersecurity specialists, and AI ethicists.

2. Higher Skill Requirements

As AI technologies develop, skill and knowledge requirements increase. This necessitates continuous learning and skill development to remain competitive in the labor market.

3. Changes in Employment Structure

New professions created by AI change the employment structure, shifting the focus from routine tasks to more complex and creative ones. This leads to the emergence of highly skilled jobs and a decrease in demand for unskilled labor.

Conclusion

AI not only replaces existing professions but also creates new opportunities and jobs requiring unique skills and approaches. These changes significantly impact the labor market and society, opening new prospects for those willing to adapt and grow with the technologies. In the following chapters, we will explore the key directions in AI education, how to work with AI, and address the ethical issues that arise, to leverage its potential for improving our lives and careers.

Chapter 4: Key Directions in AI Education

Introduction

As artificial intelligence (AI) continues to advance and integrate into various industries, the demand for skills and knowledge related to AI is growing exponentially. Education in AI is crucial for preparing the workforce of the future and ensuring that individuals can adapt to the changing job market. This chapter explores the key directions in AI education, the essential skills needed, and the strategies for acquiring and developing these skills.

Key Directions in AI Education

1. Machine Learning and Deep Learning

Machine learning (ML) and deep learning (DL) are core areas of AI that focus on creating algorithms that can learn from data and make predictions. Education in these fields covers a range of topics from basic concepts to advanced techniques.

Key Topics and Skills:

- Understanding supervised, unsupervised, and reinforcement learning
- Learning algorithms such as regression, classification, clustering, and neural networks
- Programming languages (Python, R) and libraries (TensorFlow, Keras, PyTorch)

- Practical experience with real-world datasets and problem-solving

Example Courses:

- "Machine Learning" by Andrew Ng on Coursera
- "Deep Learning Specialization" on Coursera, offered by deeplearning.ai

2. Data Science and Analytics

Data science involves extracting insights from large datasets using statistical and computational techniques. It is essential for building AI models and understanding data patterns.

Key Topics and Skills:

- Statistics and probability
- Data visualization and exploratory data analysis
- Data cleaning and preprocessing
- Tools like SQL, Excel, Tableau, and programming in Python or R

Example Courses:

- "Data Science Specialization" by Johns Hopkins University on Coursera
- "Introduction to Data Science" by IBM on edX

3. Natural Language Processing (NLP)

Natural Language Processing (NLP) focuses on the interaction between computers and human language. It is used in applications such as chatbots, language translation, and sentiment analysis.

Key Topics and Skills:

- Text preprocessing (tokenization, stemming, lemmatization)
- Language models (Bag-of-Words, TF-IDF, Word2Vec, Transformers)
- Applications of NLP in various industries
- Libraries and frameworks like NLTK, spaCy, and Hugging Face's Transformers

Example Courses:

- "Natural Language Processing Specialization" by deeplearning.ai on Coursera
- "Applied Text Mining in Python" by the University of Michigan on Coursera

4. Robotics and Autonomous Systems

Robotics involves the design, construction, and operation of robots, while autonomous systems are designed to perform tasks without human intervention.

Key Topics and Skills:

- Mechanics and electronics of robots
- Control systems and navigation
- Sensors and actuators
- Programming for robotics (C++, Python) and using platforms like ROS (Robot Operating System)

Example Courses:

- "Robotics Specialization" by the University of Pennsylvania on Coursera

- "Modern Robotics" by Northwestern University on Coursera

5. Cybersecurity for AI

As AI systems become more prevalent, ensuring their security becomes critical. Education in cybersecurity focuses on protecting AI systems from attacks and ensuring data integrity.

Key Topics and Skills:

- Fundamentals of cybersecurity (cryptography, network security)
- Threat detection and response
- Secure software development practices
- Protecting AI models and data privacy

Example Courses:

- "Cybersecurity Specialization" by the University of Maryland on Coursera
- "IBM Cybersecurity Analyst Professional Certificate" on Coursera

Strategies for Learning and Skill Development

1. Online Courses and MOOCs

Massive Open Online Courses (MOOCs) provide accessible and flexible learning opportunities for individuals looking to develop AI skills. Platforms like Coursera, edX, and Udacity offer courses from top universities and institutions.

Example: Coursera offers a wide range of AI-related courses and specializations, including machine learning, data science, and NLP.

2. Practical Projects and Competitions

Hands-on experience is crucial for mastering AI concepts. Participating in practical projects, hackathons, and competitions like Kaggle helps learners apply their knowledge to real-world problems and gain practical skills.

Example: Kaggle competitions allow participants to work on real datasets, compete with others, and learn from the community.

3. Research and Reading

Keeping up with the latest research in AI is essential for staying informed about new developments and techniques. Reading research papers, following AI conferences, and engaging with academic and industry publications can deepen understanding.

Example: arXiv.org provides access to a vast collection of research papers in AI, machine learning, and related fields.

4. Networking and Community Involvement

Joining AI communities and networks can provide support, resources, and collaboration opportunities. Engaging with peers, mentors, and professionals in the field can enhance learning and career prospects.

Example: AI and data science meetups, conferences, and online forums such as Reddit's r/MachineLearning and LinkedIn groups offer valuable networking opportunities.

Conclusion

Education in AI is vital for preparing the future workforce and ensuring that individuals can thrive in a rapidly changing job market. By focusing on key areas such as machine learning, data science, NLP, robotics, and cybersecurity, and leveraging strategies like online courses, practical projects, and community involvement, learners can develop the skills needed to succeed in the AI-driven world. In the following chapters, we will explore how to work effectively with AI, collaborate with intelligent systems, and address the ethical considerations that arise in this dynamic field.

Chapter 5: Working Together with AI

Modern artificial intelligence (AI) technologies are rapidly advancing and increasingly integrating into our daily lives and professional activities. Working with AI means not only leveraging its capabilities but also understanding how to integrate it into workflows to enhance efficiency and productivity. In this chapter, we will explore how to collaborate with AI across various fields, using its power to improve outcomes.

Benefits of Collaborating with AI

1. Increased Productivity

AI can automate routine and repetitive tasks, freeing up time for more complex and creative tasks. This allows workers to focus on strategic thinking and problem-solving, which require human intuition and creativity.

Example: In the banking sector, AI can process thousands of transactions per second, detect suspicious activities, and prevent fraud. This frees up employees to work with clients and develop new financial products.

2. Improved Decision-Making

AI algorithms can analyze vast amounts of data, identifying hidden patterns and trends that help make more informed decisions. AI can provide analytical forecasts based on data and models designed to predict future events.

Example: In healthcare, AI is used to analyze medical images and patient data, helping doctors make accurate diagnoses and develop effective treatment plans.

3. Personalized Services

AI enables the creation of personalized offers for customers based on their behavior and preferences. This improves customer experience and satisfaction, which in turn drives business growth.

Example: In e-commerce, AI analyzes customer purchase data and suggests products they might like, increasing the likelihood of a purchase and enhancing the customer experience.

Key Areas for AI Integration in the Workplace

1. Business Process Automation

Automating business processes with AI significantly reduces the time and resources spent on routine tasks. This includes automating accounting, inventory management, order processing, and other processes.

Example: In manufacturing, AI systems can manage supply chains, optimize material orders, and forecast product demand.

2. Data Processing and Analysis

AI can analyze large volumes of data, providing valuable insights and forecasts. This is especially useful in marketing, where analyzing customer behavior data helps develop effective advertising campaigns.

Example: In finance, AI is used to analyze market data and predict stock prices, helping traders make informed investment decisions.

3. Product and Service Development

AI helps develop new products and services by analyzing customer needs and market trends. This allows companies to stay competitive and adapt to market changes.

Example: In the automotive industry, AI is used to develop autonomous vehicles that can navigate roads independently, enhancing safety and convenience for users.

Tools and Platforms for Working with AI

1. Machine Learning Platforms

Various platforms and tools help develop and deploy machine learning models. These platforms provide access to libraries, visualization tools, and computational resources.

Popular Platforms:

- **TensorFlow:** An open-source machine learning library developed by Google.
- **PyTorch:** An open-source deep learning library developed by Facebook.
- **scikit-learn:** A Python library for machine learning, including tools for classification, regression, and clustering.

2. Natural Language Processing (NLP) Tools

NLP tools enable the creation of applications that can analyze and understand human language. This includes chatbots, sentiment analysis systems, and automatic translation.

Popular Tools:

- **NLTK:** A Python library for working with human language data.
- **spaCy:** An open-source NLP library designed for industrial use.
- **GPT-3:** A model by OpenAI capable of generating text and answering questions based on input data.

3. Cloud Platforms

Cloud platforms provide access to computational resources and tools for developing and deploying AI applications. They offer convenient interfaces and integration with other services.

Popular Cloud Platforms:

- **Google Cloud AI:** A platform for developing and deploying AI models by Google.
- **AWS AI Services:** A set of services by Amazon Web Services for developing AI applications.
- **Microsoft Azure AI:** A platform by Microsoft for creating and deploying AI solutions.

Examples of Successful Collaboration with AI

1. IBM Watson in Healthcare

IBM Watson is used in medical institutions to analyze medical data and suggest treatments. Doctors use Watson to diagnose complex diseases, such as cancer, and develop personalized treatment plans.

2. Chatbots in Customer Service

Many companies are implementing AI-based chatbots to improve customer service. These bots can answer frequently asked questions, help solve problems, and even process orders, freeing up employees for more complex tasks.

3. Autonomous Vehicles

Companies like Tesla and Waymo are developing autonomous vehicles that use AI for navigation and control. These cars can independently navigate roads, enhancing safety and convenience for users.

Conclusion

Collaborating with AI offers enormous opportunities to increase productivity, improve decision-making, and create personalized services. Using AI in business requires understanding its capabilities, selecting appropriate tools, and integrating them into workflows. In the following chapters, we will discuss the ethical issues related to AI use and how to prepare for future changes to maximize the potential of these technologies to improve our lives and careers.

Chapter 6: The Ethics of AI Usage

The use of artificial intelligence (AI) brings about not only technological and economic changes but also serious ethical questions. The ethics of AI encompass a wide range of aspects, including data privacy, algorithmic bias, machine autonomy, and the overall impact of AI on society. In this chapter, we will delve into the main ethical issues related to AI and discuss approaches to addressing them.

Data Privacy

1. Data Collection and Usage

AI requires large volumes of data for training and improving its models. This includes the collection of personal user data, raising privacy concerns. Unethical use of data can lead to violations of privacy rights and user security.

Example: Social networks like Facebook collect vast amounts of user data for targeted advertising. However, data breaches and unauthorized use can harm users.

Solution: Develop strict privacy policies and transparent methods for data collection and processing. Users should be informed about what data is collected and how it is used.

2. Data Protection

Cybersecurity threats and potential data breaches are serious issues. AI systems that handle sensitive data must be protected from hacking and unauthorized access.

Example: In healthcare, a leak of medical data can have serious consequences for patients.

Solution: Implement encryption methods, multi-factor authentication, and regular security audits to protect data.

Algorithmic Bias

1. Discrimination and Injustice

AI algorithms can unintentionally inherit biases from the data they are trained on. This can lead to discrimination and unfair treatment of certain groups of people.

Example: Hiring algorithms can be biased against women or ethnic minorities if the training data contains historical biases.

Solution: Use methods to test and eliminate bias in data and algorithms. Develop transparent and fair algorithms.

2. Transparency and Explainability

AI algorithms are often seen as "black boxes" whose decisions are hard to explain and understand. Lack of transparency can lead to distrust and concern among users.

Example: In the financial sector, denial of a loan based on an AI decision without an explanation can cause customer dissatisfaction.

Solution: Develop explainable AI methods that allow users to understand how and why decisions are made.

Machine Autonomy

1. Autonomous Decision-Making

Autonomous AI systems, such as self-driving cars or drones, can make decisions without human intervention. This raises questions about responsibility and safety.

Example: In the event of an accident involving a self-driving car, it is unclear who is responsible – the manufacturer, the programmers, or the AI system itself.

Solution: Develop legal frameworks and safety standards for autonomous systems. Define human rights and responsibilities in relationships with autonomous systems.

2. Ethical Dilemmas

Autonomous systems can encounter situations requiring ethical choices. For example, a self-driving car might have to choose between several potentially dangerous outcomes.

Example: A scenario where a self-driving car must decide whether to crash into a group of pedestrians or veer off the road, risking the passengers' lives.

Solution: Program AI systems with ethical principles and develop algorithms capable of making ethically justified decisions.

Impact on Society

1. Employment and Economy

The replacement of humans by machines can lead to mass unemployment and social problems. This is especially relevant for low-skilled workers whose tasks can be easily automated.

Example: Automation of production processes in factories can lead to job cuts.

Solution: Develop retraining and upskilling programs for workers whose professions are at risk of automation. Introduce social support measures.

2. Social Interaction

AI can also affect social interactions and communication. Virtual assistants and chatbots replace live communication, which can lead to isolation and reduced quality of interaction.

Example: Using chatbots for customer service can lower the level of personal interaction and cause dissatisfaction among users.

Solution: Ensure a balance between automation and personal interaction. Implement systems that support human interaction and social connections.

Conclusion

The ethics of AI usage is a complex and multifaceted topic that touches many aspects of our lives. Data privacy, algorithmic bias, machine autonomy, and societal impact all require thorough analysis and the development of approaches to address emerging issues. In the following chapters, we will explore how to prepare for future changes and use AI's potential to improve our lives and careers while adhering to ethical principles and standards.

Chapter 7: The Dangers of AI for Humanity

Artificial intelligence (AI) is a technology that promises to radically transform our world. However, these changes come with potential dangers. In this chapter, we will explore various threat scenarios, including those often depicted in popular films such as "Terminator." We will also discuss how realistic these concerns are and whether humanity should fear AI taking over the world.

Myths and Reality: "Terminator" and Other Films

Films like "Terminator" depict a bleak future where machines and AI rise against humanity, destroying or enslaving it. While these scenarios are captivating, they largely remain fiction. Let's break down several aspects of these myths and the real threats associated with AI.

1. AI Self-Awareness

A key element in films about the rise of machines is the idea that AI can gain self-awareness and act independently against human interests. In reality, modern AIs, even the most advanced ones like GPT-3, are specialized tools that perform tasks based on programming and training. They do not possess self-awareness, emotions, or goals beyond those programmed by developers.

2. Control and Security

In films, machines often gain full control over weapon systems and infrastructure, using this against humans. In real life, the security and control of AI systems are top priorities for developers. There are strict protocols and safety measures in place to prevent unauthorized access to critical systems. For example, autonomous weapon systems are under strict control and monitoring to prevent accidental or intentional malfunctions.

Real Threats and Challenges of AI

While scenarios from films like "Terminator" are unlikely, real threats and challenges associated with AI require attention and regulation.

1. Automation and Unemployment

The automation of jobs through AI can lead to significant unemployment, especially among low-skilled workers. Job losses can cause economic and social problems, such as increased inequality and instability.

Example: Studies show that up to 47% of all jobs in the U.S. could be automated in the next few decades.

2. Ethical and Legal Issues

AI can be used to create surveillance systems that violate privacy rights. Additionally, autonomous systems such as drones and robots may face ethical dilemmas that are difficult to program.

Example: The use of facial recognition systems for mass surveillance raises serious privacy and civil liberty concerns.

3. Cybersecurity

AI can be used to create powerful cyberweapons capable of causing significant harm. The automation of cyberattacks and the development of advanced hacking methods can render traditional defense methods ineffective.

Example: In 2017, the WannaCry ransomware attack, which used exploits developed with the help of AI, affected thousands of computers worldwide, including healthcare and infrastructure systems.

Regulation and Prevention of Threats

To prevent potential threats associated with AI, appropriate regulatory and control measures are necessary. Here are several strategies that can help:

1. Regulation and Laws

Develop international and national laws regulating the use of AI in critical systems. This includes controlling autonomous weapons, surveillance systems, and protecting privacy rights.

Example: The European Union has developed strict rules for the use of AI, including requirements for transparency and accountability for AI system developers.

2. Ethical Standards

Create ethical standards for the development and use of AI. This includes preventing algorithmic bias, protecting data privacy, and ensuring the fair use of technology.

Example: The IEEE has developed the "Ethically Aligned Design" initiative, which calls for the creation of transparent and fair algorithms.

3. Education and Awareness

Increase AI awareness and education for the general public and professionals. This helps better understand the potential and limitations of AI and how to protect against its negative consequences.

Example: Universities and educational platforms like Coursera and edX offer courses on AI ethics and cybersecurity.

Conclusion

While scenarios from films like "Terminator" are unlikely, real threats associated with AI require serious attention and regulation. Data privacy, cybersecurity, ethics, and the impact on employment are all important issues that need to be addressed for the safe and effective use of AI. Humanity should not fear AI but work towards its safe integration into society to leverage its potential for improving lives and overcoming global challenges.

Chapter 8: Apocalypse by AI. Is an AI-Induced End of the World Possible and What to Do in Case It Happens?

The idea of an apocalypse caused by artificial intelligence (AI) has long been confined to the realm of science fiction. However, with the advancement of technologies and the increasing integration of AI into various aspects of life, such scenarios have become a subject of serious discussion among scientists, philosophers, and technology experts. In this chapter, we will examine how realistic these threats are, possible end-of-the-world scenarios caused by AI, and what can be done to prevent them.

The AI Apocalypse Perspective

1. The Threat of Superintelligence

One of the main fears associated with AI is the possibility of creating a superintelligence – a machine that surpasses human intelligence in all areas. Such an AI could become unpredictable and uncontrollable, making decisions that might threaten humanity's existence.

Example: Philosopher Nick Bostrom discusses possible scenarios where superintelligence might solve problems without considering human values, leading to catastrophic consequences. For instance, an AI programmed to

maximize the production of paperclips might destroy
humanity to use Earth's resources to achieve its goal.

2. Autonomous Weapon Systems

Military AI technologies could pose a serious threat,
especially if they gain autonomous capabilities. Without
proper control, such systems could make erroneous
decisions or be used by malicious actors to carry out
attacks.

Example: Autonomous drones and robot soldiers
designed for combat might become uncontrollable or be
hacked, leading to uncontrolled violence and destruction.

3. AI Failures and Errors

AI integrated into critical infrastructures such as power
grids, transportation systems, and financial markets could
become sources of massive failures and catastrophic
errors. Programming errors or unexpected situations could
result in irreversible consequences.

Example: In 2010, a "Flash Crash" occurred in the US
stock market when algorithmic trading led to a sudden
market collapse, demonstrating how even relatively simple
AI systems can cause serious disruptions.

Real Threats and Challenges

While AI apocalypse scenarios seem unlikely, they raise
important questions about AI safety and ethics. Let's
examine real threats and how they can be prevented:

1. Developing Safe AI

Creating safe and ethically sound AI is a crucial task for developers and researchers. This includes designing algorithms that consider human values and prevent uncontrollable AI behavior.

Solution: Research projects like "AI Alignment" from OpenAI aim to create methods and algorithms that ensure AI aligns with human values and ethical principles.

2. International Regulation and Control

There is a need to develop international norms and rules regulating the development and use of AI, especially in military and critical infrastructure. This can help prevent arms races and technology misuse.

Solution: Organizations like the United Nations are working on international agreements regulating the use of autonomous weapon systems and other dangerous technologies.

3. Education and Awareness

Increasing AI awareness and education helps society better understand the potential and risks associated with these technologies. This also includes preparing specialists who can work on AI safety and ethics.

Solution: Universities and educational platforms should offer courses on AI ethics, cybersecurity, and risk management related to AI.

Actions in Case of Apocalyptic Scenarios

If an AI-induced apocalypse threat arises, it is essential to have an action plan to minimize consequences and protect humanity:

1. Monitoring and Early Warning

Develop monitoring and early warning systems for potential AI threats. These systems can analyze AI behavior and identify anomalies indicating uncontrollable behavior.

Example: Using big data analysis and predictive analytics to track AI activity and identify potential threats.

2. Contingency Plans and Response Measures

Develop contingency plans and response measures in case of threats. This includes creating specialized teams that can quickly respond to incidents and mitigate threats.

Example: Establishing national and international agencies similar to FEMA in the US to respond to AI-related emergencies.

3. Collaborative Efforts and Cooperation

International cooperation and information exchange between countries and organizations can help respond more effectively to threats and develop precautionary measures.

Example: Joint research and development in AI safety conducted by international consortia and scientific communities.

Conclusion

While scenarios of an AI apocalypse, like those in films such as "Terminator," are unlikely, real threats associated with AI require serious attention and precautionary measures. Developing safe and ethical AI, international regulation, and education are key elements in preventing potential catastrophes. Humanity should not fear AI but work towards its safe integration into society to leverage its potential for improving life and overcoming global challenges.

Conclusion

Artificial intelligence (AI) represents one of humanity's most significant achievements. Its potential to transform various aspects of our lives is virtually limitless. However, with these opportunities come significant challenges. In this book, we have explored many aspects of AI, from its ability to replace traditional professions to the potential threats it may pose.

Prospects and Challenges

AI has immense potential to increase productivity, improve the quality of life, and create new opportunities. In areas such as medicine, finance, education, and transportation, AI is already showing impressive results, helping people tackle tasks that once seemed impossible.

However, along with these advancements, there are significant challenges. The replacement of professions and job automation can lead to mass unemployment, especially among low-skilled workers. This requires adaptation and retraining to remain relevant in the changing job market.

Ethical Issues

The ethics of AI usage is one of the key topics. Data privacy, algorithmic bias, machine autonomy, and the societal impact of AI all require thorough analysis and the development of approaches to address emerging issues. We discussed the importance of creating ethical algorithms, protecting user data, and developing international norms and rules for AI regulation.

Real Threats and Their Prevention

Scenarios of an AI apocalypse, like those in films such as "Terminator," are unlikely, but real threats associated with AI require serious attention. This includes cybersecurity, control over autonomous weapon systems, and preventing failures in critical infrastructures. International cooperation and the development of precautionary measures will help prevent potential catastrophes.

The Future of AI

The future of AI promises to be exciting and full of opportunities. As technologies develop, we can expect smarter systems that help us solve complex problems, improve our quality of life, and open new horizons. However, to achieve this, it is necessary to prepare for future changes, develop the necessary skills and knowledge, and actively participate in forming ethical and legal norms for the safe use of AI.

Final Thoughts

AI is a powerful tool that can significantly improve our lives, but it also requires a responsible approach. We must strive to use AI for the benefit of humanity while recognizing and addressing the emerging risks and ethical issues. Only in this way can we create a future where AI becomes a reliable assistant and ally, not a threat.

Thank you for joining us on this journey through the world of AI. We hope this book has helped you better understand the potential and challenges associated with artificial intelligence and prepare for future changes.

I would like to express my deepest gratitude to everyone who has supported and encouraged me throughout the journey of writing this book. Your insights, feedback, and unwavering support have been invaluable.

To my family and friends, thank you for your patience and understanding as I dedicated countless hours to this project.

To my colleagues and mentors, your expertise and guidance have been instrumental in shaping the ideas presented in this book. Lastly, to my readers, thank you for your interest and engagement.

I hope this book inspires you to explore the possibilities and challenges of artificial intelligence and to contribute to a future where technology enhances our lives.

Best regards,
Serhii Maley

www.ingramcontent.com/pod-product-compliance
Lightning Source LLC
LaVergne TN
LVHW051623050326
832903LV00033B/4633